HOCKEY
MATH AT THE RINK

⌃⌐ BY TOM ROBINSON

Published by The Child's World®
1980 Lookout Drive • Mankato, MN 56003-1705
800-599-READ • www.childsworld.com

Acknowledgments
The Child's World®: Mary Berendes, Publishing Director
The Design Lab: Design and production
Red Line Editorial: Editorial direction

Photographs ©: Shutterstock Images, Cover, Title, 29; Elise
Amendola/AP Images, 4-5; Anthony Nesmith/AP Images,
6–7; Scott Prokop/Shutterstock Images, 8–9; Jerry S.
Mendoza/AP Images, 10–11; Mark J. Terrill/AP Images,
12–13; Josh Holmberg/AP Images, 14, 22–23; Reinhold
Matay/AP Images, 17; Chris Szagola/AP Images,
18; Bettmann/Corbis/AP Images, 21; Patrick Tuohy/
Shutterstock Images, 24; AP Images, 27

ISBN 9781614734109
LCCN 2012946505

Printed in the United States of America
Mankato, MN
November, 2012
PA02144

ABOUT THE AUTHOR

Tom Robinson is the author of 33 books, including 25 about sports. The Susquehanna, Pennsylvania, native is an award-winning sportswriter and former newspaper sports editor.

TABLE OF CONTENTS

Atlanta Thrashers goalie Kari Lehtonen (32) makes a save on a shot by Boston Bruins' Brad Boyes (26) during a shootout on March 21, 2006.

MATH ON THE RINK

All losses are not equal in hockey. Teams at least get some reward for being tied when time runs out. In the National Hockey League (NHL), tie games go to overtime. Sometimes a **shootout** happens if the game is still tied after overtime. Teams receive a point in the league **standings** for losing in overtime or a shootout.

Math helps us understand and enjoy hockey. The sport has its own **statistic**. It is the plus/minus rating. Goal and **assist** totals are tracked for scorers. An **average** or **percentage** tells how well goalies perform.

There are many interesting and fun ways to look at the numbers. Use your math skills as you take a look at hockey. You'll be surprised at how much they are needed!

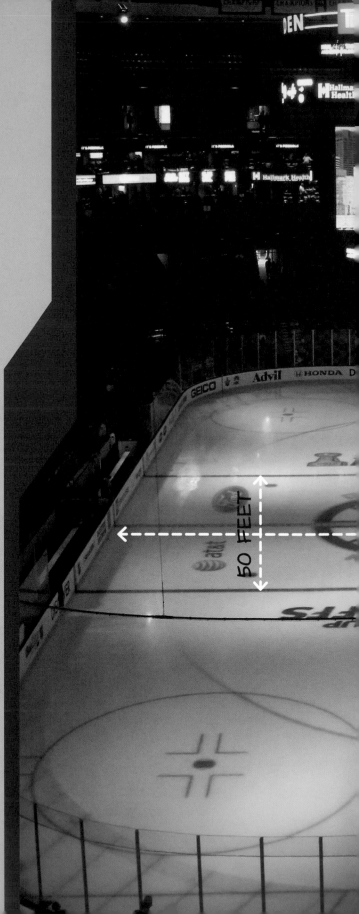

The Rink

The Boston Bruins moved to a new home in 1995. At the same time they lost a home-ice edge. When the TD Garden opened, the old Boston Garden closed. The Boston Garden was built when the NHL did not have standard rink sizes. It was a smaller rink. The surface was 191 feet long by 83 feet wide. Teams had to adjust to the rink's smaller space when they came to Boston.

All NHL rinks are now 200 feet long and 85 feet wide. There are other sizes, though, in other levels of hockey. Larger rinks are used for international play. They are 200 feet by 98 feet.

All hockey rinks include a red line at center ice. They also have two blue lines. Each team has an offensive zone. It goes from the blue line to the end of the rink. There is also a neutral zone. The neutral zone is the center-ice area between the blue lines. It includes the red line. It is 85 feet by 50 feet in the NHL.

Find the perimeter and area of the neutral zone. Perimeter is the distance around an object. Area is the amount of surface space of a shape.

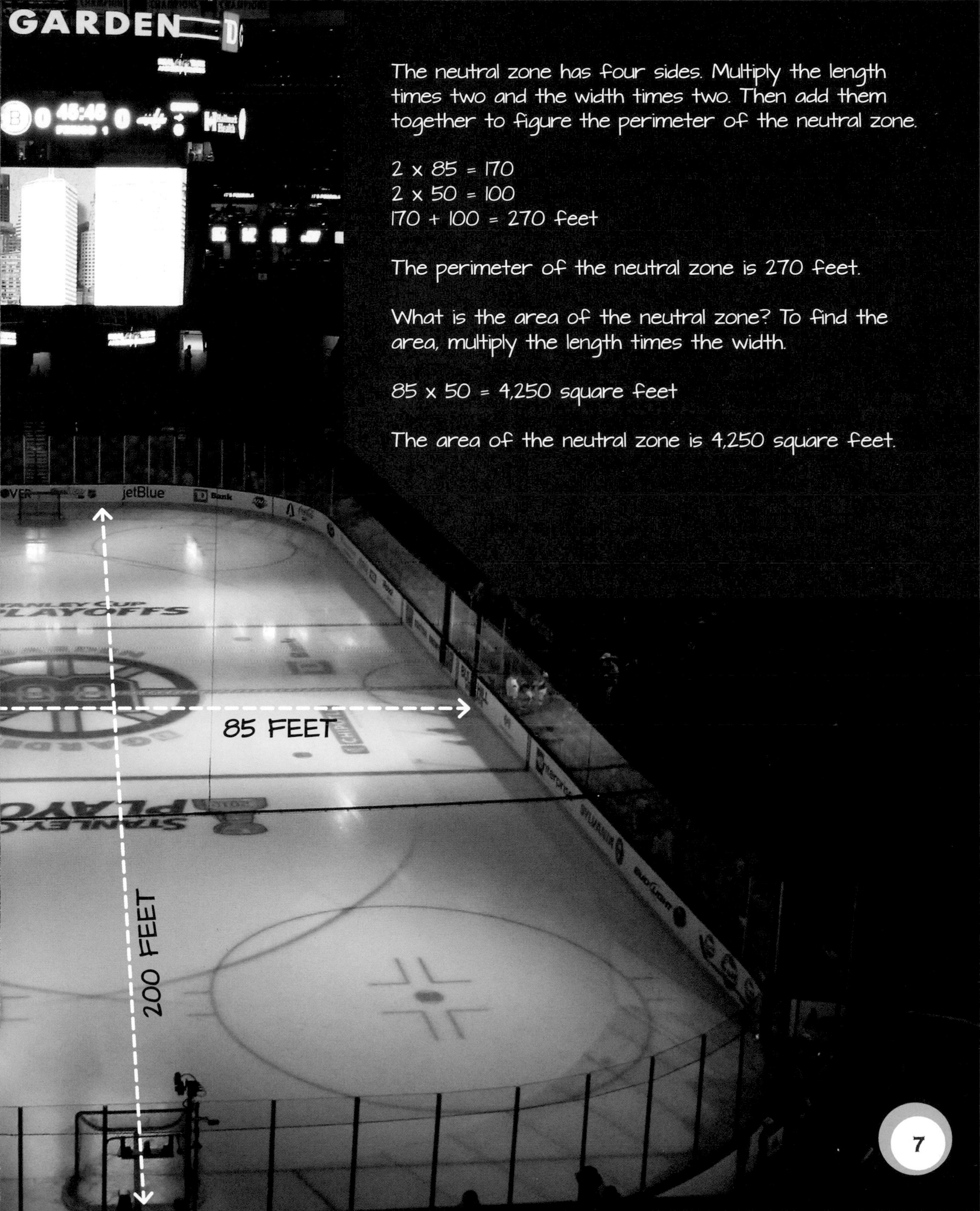

The neutral zone has four sides. Multiply the length times two and the width times two. Then add them together to figure the perimeter of the neutral zone.

2 x 85 = 170
2 x 50 = 100
170 + 100 = 270 feet

The perimeter of the neutral zone is 270 feet.

What is the area of the neutral zone? To find the area, multiply the length times the width.

85 x 50 = 4,250 square feet

The area of the neutral zone is 4,250 square feet.

85 FEET

200 FEET

Standings

Winning the most games is not the only way to come out on top in an NHL season. Losing the right way also helps.

Hockey has its own way of figuring out **standings**. Football, basketball, baseball, and most other sports rank teams by wins and winning percentage. While there are ties in college hockey as well as some lower levels, there are none in the NHL. The NHL gives two points for a win and one for an overtime or shootout loss.

The 2011-12 NHL Pacific Division standings were:

TEAM	WINS	LOSSES	OT LOSSES	TOTAL POINTS
Phoenix Coyotes	42	27	13	97
San Jose Sharks	43	29	10	96
Los Angeles Kings	40	27	15	95
Dallas Stars	42	35	5	89
Anaheim Ducks	34	36	12	80

Phoenix Coyotes and Los Angeles Kings players line up on the ice during the national anthem before a game on March 20, 2008 in Phoenix, Arizona.

How do you figure out the total points?
Wins are worth two points. Overtime
and shootout losses are worth one point.

total points = (2 x number of wins) +
number of overtime/shootout losses

Now use the Phoenix Coyotes standings
numbers in the formula:

2 x 42 = 84
84 + 13 = 97

Phoenix had 97 total points.

Detroit Red Wings defenseman Nicklas Lidstrom takes a shot on goal during a power play against the Florida Panthers on September 24, 2006.

Penalty Time

Players are sent to the **penalty** box when they commit penalties in hockey. Players get penalties for different reasons. Tripping, hooking, and interference are examples of minor penalties that send players to the penalty box for two minutes. There are also major penalties, such as for fighting. Major penalties cost the player five minutes. Misconduct penalties can send a player out for ten minutes or the rest of the game.

When one team has a player in the penalty box, the other team has a power play. Two of the most important team statistics in hockey are power-play and penalty-killing percentages. Percentage tells how many times out of 100 an event occurs. Teams are measured by how often they take advantage of having an extra skater and how well they stop a power play.

The Philadelphia Flyers led the NHL in power-play goals with 66. The Flyers had 335 chances. What was their percentage?

To find the percentage, divide goals by the chances. Then, multiply the number by 100.

$66 \div 315 = .1970$
$.1970 \times 100 = 19.7$

The Flyers had a 19.7 power-play percentage.

Three teams scored on more than 20 percent of power plays in the 2011–12 NHL regular season. The Nashville Predators scored on 54 of 250 chances. This led the league with 21.6 percent. The San Jose Sharks scored 57 times in 270 chances for 21.1 percent. The Edmonton Oilers scored on 54 of 262, or 20.6 percent. The New Jersey Devils allowed 27 power-play goals in 259 chances. The Devils killed 232 chances out of 259, or 89.6 percent (232 divided by 259). That was the best in the NHL.

Taking Shifts

A hockey team can dump the puck into the corner of its offensive end. This is a chance for the team to change players. Hockey uses substitutions more than any other major sport. As one line heads to the bench, another line climbs over the boards. The teammates join the action as play continues.

Forwards include a center and wings on each side. They rotate in three or four groups of three players called a line. **Defensemen** play two at a time. They often move in and out of the lineup in three pairs.

Playing time does not come out exactly equal for each player. But it is split up much more evenly than in other sports. The length of a shift changes, but most are well under a minute.

New Jersey Devils right wing Dainius Zubrus (8) carries the puck up the ice in Game 3 of the NHL Stanley Cup Finals on June 4, 2012.

The Los Angeles Kings and New Jersey Devils each used 18 skaters in Game 3 of the Stanley Cup Finals on June 4, 2012. The Kings won the game, 4–0.

Every New Jersey skater was on the ice for at least nine minutes. Marek Zidlicky played the most at 21 minutes and 48 seconds.

Los Angeles used four defensemen for between 20 and 26 minutes. All other skaters played between 6 minutes 48 seconds and 19 minutes 32 seconds.

12

How many shifts of forwards could a coach use in a 20-minute period in shifts of 30 seconds? How about 48 seconds?

To find out, divide the total time by the length of shifts. This is easier if you change minutes into seconds. To change minutes into seconds, multiply the minutes by 60.

20 minutes x 60 = 1,200 seconds

There are 1,200 seconds in each 20-minute period. If the average shift is 30 seconds, there would be 40 shifts per period:

1,200 ÷ 30 = 40 shifts

If the average shift is 48 seconds, there would be 25 shifts.

1,200 ÷ 48 = 25 shifts

Boston Bruins center Patrice Bergeron (37) led the NHL in plus/minus with +36 in the 2011-12 season.

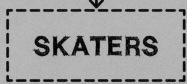

SKATERS

The Perfect Statistic

Hockey players have been measured for decades by a simple statistic. That statistic is the plus/minus. It is just now making its way into basketball and other sports.

Plus/minus measures a player in a simple way. Players are judged based on how their team does when they are on the ice. They get a plus for each goal their team scores and a minus for each goal scored against them.

Power-play goals do not count in plus/minus. Neither do shorthanded goals.

Plus/minus ratings are shown with a positive or negative number. Roman Hamrlik was +8 for the Washington Capitals and Barret Jackman was -8 for the St. Louis Blues during the 2012 Stanley Cup playoffs.

When two negative numbers are compared, the higher number has the least value. Looking at a number line can help show this. On a number line, numbers on the left have less value than numbers on the right. So -8 is less than -4, but 8 (or +8) is greater than 4 (or +4).

Joe Corvo played five games for the Boston Bruins against the Washington Capitals in the 2012 Stanley Cup playoffs. Corvo went +1 in each of the first four games and -1 in the fifth game. What was his total plus/minus for the series?

$$1 + 1 + 1 + 1 - 1 = + 3$$

Corvo was +3 total.

Goals

Players not only need to put the puck past a goalie to score. They also need to keep the shot between the posts and below the crossbar that defines the top of the net. The crossbar is set 4 feet above the ice. The length of the goal from post to post is 6 feet.

What is the area of the goal?

$6 \times 4 = 24$

The area of the goal is 24 square feet. That is the target that scorers need to make and goalies need to protect.

The top goal scorers in the NHL in the 2011-12 regular season were:

PLAYER	TEAM	GOALS	TEAM GOALS	PLAYER SHOTS ON GOAL
Steven Stamkos	Tampa Bay Lightning	60	232	303
Evgeni Malkin	Pittsburgh Penguins	50	273	339
Marian Gaborik	New York Rangers	41	222	276

There are different ways to look at the top goal-scorers. One way is to compare who scored the highest percentage of the team's goals. Another is to compare who scored goals on the greatest percentage of shots on goal.

Stamkos scored 60 of his team's 232 goals. What percentage is that?

$60 \div 232 = .2586$

Stamkos scored 25.9 percent of the team's goals. Malkin scored 18.3 percent of Pittsburgh's goals. Gaborik had 18.5 percent of the Rangers' goals.

Stamkos scored on 60 of his 303 shots on goal. What percentage is that?

$60 \div 303 = .1980$

Stamkos scored 19.8 percent of his shots on goal. Malkin's shooting percentage was 14.7. Gaborik's was 14.9. Again, Stamkos was the best.

Tampa Bay Lightning center Steven Stamkos skates during a game against the Carolina Hurricanes on December 31, 2011.

Philadelphia Flyers right wing Claude Giroux passes the puck during a game against the New Jersey Devils on November 3, 2011.

Assists

Pavel Datsyuk passes to Detroit Red Wings teammate Ian White. White takes a shot. The shot is deflected into the net by fellow Red Wing Johan Franzen. In this play, White gets an assist for sending the puck to Franzen. Datsyuk gets the second assist for passing to White.

The scoring rules of hockey honor teamwork. Up to two assists are awarded on each goal. Assists are also given to players who have their shots stopped before a teammate scores on a rebound.

Vancouver's Henrik Sedin led the NHL with 67 regular-season assists in 2011–12. Philadelphia's Claude Giroux was second with 65.

While there are up to two assists on any goal, some goals have single assists and some have none.

Here are the total goals and assists for NHL Atlantic Division teams in 2011-12:

Team	Goals	Assists
New York Rangers	222	387
Pittsburgh Penguins	273	473
Philadelphia Flyers	260	450
New Jersey Devils	216	373
New York Islanders	196	348

To find the average number of assists per goal, divide the assists by the number of goals. How many assists per goal did the New York Rangers have?

The team had 387 assists for their 222 goals.

$$387 \div 222 = 1.743$$

The Rangers had 1.74 assists for every goal.

Points

Assists help decide scoring titles. Goals and assists each count as one point for the player. A player with four goals and three assists has seven points.

4 + 3 = 7

Wayne Gretzky led the NHL in scoring 11 times in 15 seasons from 1979-80 through 1993-94. He was the only player ever to score more than 200 points in a season.

The total needed to win the scoring title has not been above 125 since the start of the 21st century. Here is a look at the scoring race by decade since the 1949-50 season. That is when the league started playing schedules consisting of at least 70 games:

DECADE*	MOST FREQUENT LEADERS	WINNING POINT TOTALS EACH YEAR	AVERAGE WINNING TOTAL	CHANGE FROM PREVIOUS
1950s	Gordie Howe	78, 86, 86, 95, 81, 75, 88, 89, 84, 96	85.8	NA
1960s	Stan Mikita	81, 95, 84, 86, 89, 87, 97, 97, 87, 126	92.9	+7.1
1970s	Phil Esposito	120, 152, 133, 130, 145, 135, 125, 136, 132, 134	134.2	+41.3
1980s	Wayne Gretzky	137, 164, 212, 196, 205, 208, 215, 183, 168, 199	188.7	+54.5
1990s	Mario Lemieux	142, 163, 131, 160, 130, 161, 122, 102, 127	137.6	-51.1
2000s	Jaromir Jagr	96, 121, 96, 106, 94, 125, 120, 112, 113	109.2	-28.4
2010s	Henrik Sedin, Daniel Sedin, Evgeni Malkin	112, 104, 109	108.3	-0.9

*By year that season finished. Strike-shortened 1994-95 season is not included. NHL did not play in 2004-05.

To figure the average winning point total of the 1950s, add the yearly totals and divide by the number of years.

78 + 86 + 86 + 95 + 81 + 75 + 88 + 89 + 84 + 96 = 858

858 ÷ 10 = 85.8

In the 1950s, scoring champions had an average of
85.8 points per game. The high point was in the 1980s.
The scoring champion averaged 188.7 points per season.
The average total needed to win a scoring title has gone
down for three straight decades.

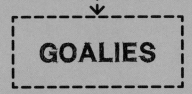

GOALIES

Statistics

There are three statistics by which most goalies are judged. Shutouts involve simple counting. A goalie gets a shutout each time he or she plays an entire game without letting the opponent score.

Before leading the Los Angeles Kings to the Stanley Cup title, Jonathan Quick led the NHL during the 2011–12 regular season with ten shutouts.

Save percentage reflects the percentage of shots on goal that a goalie is able to stop. Save percentages are shown as three-digit numbers that start with a decimal point. To find this number, divide the saves by the shots.

St. Louis Blues goalie Brian Elliott makes a glove save during a game against the Los Angeles Kings on March 22, 2012.

Brian Elliott of the St. Louis Blues saved 914 of 972 shots against him.

914 ÷ 972 = .940

He had a .940 save percentage.

Jussi Markkanen of the New York Rangers guards the goal in a game against the Calgary Flames on January 5, 2004.

Goals-against average (GAA) is the number of goals allowed based on an average 60-minute game. In its simplest form, a goalie who allows ten goals in four full 60-minute games would have a 2.50 GAA, because $10 \div 4 = 2.50$.

If the time played is not divisible by 60, another step is needed. A goalie who allowed 5 goals in 185 minutes would need the number of goals allowed multiplied by 60 before being divided by 185. The GAA in that that case would be:

$5 \times 60 = 300$

$300 \div 185 = 1.62$

The GAA would be 1.62.

Most goalies do not play an even number of minutes. In that case, time played needs to be converted to seconds.

60 minutes $\times 60$ seconds in a minute $= 3,600$

There are 3,600 seconds in a game.

Goals have to be multiplied by 3,600. Then that number is divided by seconds played to determine the GAA.

What are the GAAs for the goalies in the chart? Each had even numbers of minutes played.

Player	Minutes	Goals
Johnson	498	14
Kovlov	500	17
Pierre	493	15

What is the GAA for Johnson?

$14 \times 60 = 840$

$840 \div 498 = 1.69$ GAA

What is the GAA for Kovlov?

$17 \times 60 = 1,020$

$1,020 \div 500 = 2.04$

What is Pierre's GAA?

$15 \times 60 = 900$

$900 \div 493 = 1.86$

Career Path

Through the end of the 2011-12 season, only two goalies in NHL history had shutouts in 100 or more regular-season games.

Terry Sawchuk had 103 shutouts from 1950 to 1970. He played for Detroit, Boston, Toronto, Los Angeles, and the New York Rangers.

Martin Brodeur, who began his New Jersey Devils career in 1992, passed Sawchuk in the 2009-10 season. His total reached 119 in 2011-12.

This double line graph shows the shutouts per season based on Sawchuk's and Brodeur's ages at the end of each season.

One goalie had more shutouts before age 30. The other goalie had more after age 30. Who had the advantage in each? What was the highest number of shutouts by either goalie in a season? At what ages did each goalie have the biggest increase?

Sawchuk had the advantage before age 30 and Brodeur after 30. Add all the values from the graph. This shows that Sawchuk led 76-55 through age 29. Brodeur led 64-27 from age 30 on. The best total was 12. Sawchuk did it three times; Brodeur once. Sawchuk went up 10 (from 1 to 11) at age 21. Brodeur went up 7 (from 5 to 12) at age 34.

YEARLY SHUTOUTS (BY AGE)
MARTIN BRODEUR VS. TERRY SAWCHUK

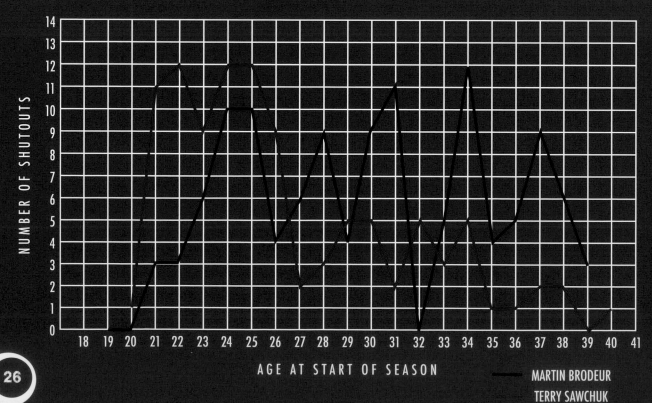

NUMBER OF SHUTOUTS

AGE AT START OF SEASON

—— MARTIN BRODEUR
TERRY SAWCHUK

Detroit Red Wings goalie Terry Sawchuk guards the goal in November 1959.

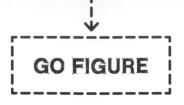

1. A hockey team has 50 wins and 10 overtime losses in a season. What were the team's total points?

2. Jim Craig saved 163 of 178 shots as goalie of the 1980 U.S. Olympic Team's "Miracle on Ice." What was Craig's save percentage?

3. The New Jersey Devils had 216 goals and 373 assists in the 2011–12 season. What was the team's average number of assists per goal?

4. A goalie allowed eight goals in six 60-minute games. What is his GAA?

Answer Key

1. 50 x 2 = 100
   100 + 10 = **110 total points**

2. 163 ÷ 178 = **.916 save percentage**

3. 373 ÷ 216 = **1.73 assists per goal**

4. 8 ÷ 6 = **1.33 GAA**

Brad Richards of Canada controls the puck against Alexander Ovechkin of the Russian Federation during a game at the Winter Olympics in Turin, Italy, on February 22, 2006.

assist (uh-SISST): An assist is a pass that sets up a goal. Assist totals are tracked for scorers.

average (AV-uh-rij): An average is found by adding up a group of figures and then dividing the total by the number of figures added. The Rangers had an average of 1.74 assists for every goal.

defensemen (di-FENS-men): Defensemen are players who protect the goalie and prevent goals. Hockey teams use two defensemen at a time.

penalty (PEN-uhl-tee): A penalty is a punishment that a team or player suffers for breaking the rules. Players are sent to the penalty box when they commit fouls in hockey.

percentage (pur-SEN-tij): A percentage is a number out of a hundred. The Flyers had a 19.7 power-play percentage in the 2011–12 NHL season.

standings (STAN-dingz): Standings are the positions or rankings of all teams within a league during a regular season of play. Teams receive a point in the league standings for losing in overtime.

statistic (stuh-TISS-tik): A statistic is a fact or piece of information expressed in a number or percentage. The plus/minus rating is a hockey statistic.

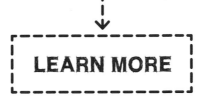

LEARN MORE

Books

Greve, Tom. *Hockey Goalies.* Vero Beach, FL: Rourke, 2010.

Mahaney, Ian F. *The Math of Hockey.* New York: PowerKids Press, 2011.

Stubbs, Dave. *Our Game: The History of Hockey in Canada.* Montréal, Canada: Lobster Press, 2006.

Web Sites

Visit our Web site for links about hockey math:
childsworld.com/links

Note to Parents, Teachers, and Librarians: We routinely verify our Web links to make sure they are safe and active sites. So encourage your readers to check them out!

INDEX